The Sayings of James Joyce

The Sayings of

JAMES
JOYCE

edited by
SEAN SHEEHAN

DUCKWORTH

First published in 1995 by
Gerald Duckworth & Co. Ltd.
The Old Piano Factory
48 Hoxton Square, London N1 6PB
Tel: 0171 729 5986
Fax: 0171 729 0015

Introduction and editorial arrangement
© 1995 by Sean Sheehan

A catalogue record for this book is available
from the British Library

ISBN 0 7156 2637 X

Typeset by Ray Davies
Printed in Great Britain by
Redwood Books Ltd., Trowbridge

Contents

Introduction

James Joyce had a strange and singular life. Born in 1882 into a middle-class family determined to provide him with the best education possible, he became the youngest-ever pupil at Clongowes Wood College – aged 'half past six' as he stated to his new masters at Ireland's most prestigious school, run by the equally distinguished Jesuits. As it turned out, these early years were destined to provide one of the few stable periods in his entire life; financial insecurity and long battles to get his work published would bedevil much of his future, and when money ceased to be a problem he faced the ordeal of coping with his daughter's severe mental illness.

Joyce had been at Clongowes for less than a year when the nationalist leader Charles Stuart Parnell was denounced by the Catholic Church and members of his own party for daring to breach the accepted code of sexual behaviour. The event came to represent for Joyce his country's hypocrisy and repression, as well as foreshadowing his own family's personal decline into debt and turmoil. In the years that followed the young James found that each change of address signalled a further decline in fortune and social esteem, which then – as now – was marked by moving from the south of Dublin to north of the city.

He entered University College at sixteen, a poor but brilliant student who paid scant attention to the formal syllabus. His only close relationships were with his brother Stanislaus, and with John Bryne (Cranly in *A Portrait of the Artist as a Young Man*) whom he met at university. His relations with most other people ranged from the disdainful to the outright contemptuous, and he was unmoved by the rising tide of Irish cultural nationalism; while writers such as W.B. Yeats embraced the movement, writing books like *The Celtic Twilight*,

Joyce was learning Norwegian so that he could read
Ibsen in the original. His feelings towards Ireland,
however, were far more complicated than a first reading
of the autobiographical *A Portrait of the Artist as a Young
Man* might suggest. The novel does come to a climax
with the decision to leave Ireland, but the young artist
also speaks of forging the 'uncreated conscience' of his
race, and the self-dramatising arrogance of a young man
who too proudly rejects the 'cultic twalette' is treated
with a healthy dose of irony. An early draft of his first
novel has survived in parts. It was written in 1904-5, is
far more autobiographical, and has been published as
Stephen Hero.

After leaving Ireland Joyce spent the next ten years in
Trieste, apart from a short spell in Rome. He heartily
disliked Rome, but it may have been the experience of
working there in a bank that conditioned his feelings
and, apart from teaching in language schools and giving
private lessons when strapped for cash, he never again
worked for anyone else. He lived through the First
World War in neutral Zurich, and after a short return to
Trieste he left for Paris where he spent most of the rest of
his life. 1939 saw the outbreak of the Second World War
and the publication of *Finnegans Wake*. Joyce was driven
back to Zurich for safety and died there in 1941.

Joyce initially left Ireland from economic necessity as
well as ideological conviction, but when, years later, he
was financially independent – Harriet Weaver gave him
today's equivalent of at least half a million pounds with
no strings attached – his refusal to consider returning
had a lot to do with his steadfast rejection of the Catholic
Church's hold over the newly independent Ireland. The
stultifying conservatism of the new State was anathema
to Joyce; for a variety of connected reasons – artistic,
personal, social and political – he knew that he would
not return: the spirit of Ireland recorded in his collection
of short stories, *Dubliners*, had if anything grown more
repressive and disillusioning. Joyce is often portrayed as
apolitical, but this is too simple and ultimately
misleading. The library of books he left behind in Trieste
when he moved to Paris in 1920 contained classic

anarchist texts by Bakunin and Kropotkin, and his
refusal to marry was always a political statement; when
he finally consented to a register office marriage in 1931
it was purely for family reasons. His indifference to
national politics remained ideological, and his feelings
about Ireland developed into a complex mix of nostalgia
and anger. He was often asked why he did not return to
Ireland, and one of his few recorded replies was 'Have I
ever left it?'. Ireland's attitude towards Joyce, on the
other hand, has been a classic case of cultural
expropriation, and the benign face of the author that
now graces the country's £10 note has been carefully
doctored to present a kindly old gent, smiling
indulgently.

It is difficult to recognise on the banknote the man
who consistently refused to exchange his British
passport for an Irish one or the angry young man who
left his country's shore in 1904 with Nora Barnacle. Joyce
and Nora remained together until his death in 1941, fully
justifying the comment of Joyce's father when he first
heard her name ('she'll stick with him'). They first met
on 10 June 1904 on a Dublin street and first went out
together six days later, a date enshrined in world
literature as the day in the life of Leopold Bloom – the
fictional hero of *Ulysses* – and Stephen Dedalus and
Molly Bloom plus the whole host of minor characters
who make up the human world of *Ulysses*. Early
admirers of the novel were struck by the author's
mastery of language, and Frank Budgen, one of the few
friends Joyce confided in, once enquired about how the
writing of *Ulysses* was proceeding. Joyce replied that he
had been working hard on it all day. 'Does that mean
you've written a great deal?' asked Budgen reasonably.
'Two sentences' was the reply, and Budgen assumed
that he had been looking for the right word, the *mot
juste*. 'No,' said Joyce, 'I have the words already. What I
am seeking is the perfect order of words in the sentence.
There is an order in every way appropriate. I think I
have it.' Joyce was working on an episode in which he
wanted to bring in a seduction theme, and the final
order of the words emerged as 'Perfume of embraces all

him assailed. With hungered flesh obscurely, he mutely craved to adore.' The same attention to detail emerges in a letter he wrote to his aunt Josephine in 1921. 'Is it possible,' he enquires, 'for an ordinary person to climb over the area railings of no. 7 Eccles Street, either from the path or the steps, lower himself from the lowest part of the railings till his feet are within 2 feet or 3 of the ground and drop unhurt? I saw it done myself but by a man of rather athletic build. I require this information in detail in order to determine the wording of a paragraph.' Joyce continued writing to his aunt for 'any news you like, programmes, pawntickets, press cuttings, handbills. I like reading them.' Joyce later claimed that the *unused* notes for *Ulysses* weighed twelve kilos!

Early admirers like Ezra Pound, who saw the work of *Ulysses* unfold in published episodes, began to think he was becoming obsessed with language and felt that their fears were indeed more than justified when instalments of *Finnegans Wake* appeared. In a way, though, it was a logical progression when one considers that the author of 'The Dead', the culminating story of *Dubliners* and arguably the most perfect short story in English, was only 25 at the time of its composition. Joyce had quickly exhausted conventional narrative and traditional storytelling, but the need to write imaginative fiction could not be simply laid aside. He wrote poetry, but it was never more than occasional; the early *Chamber Music* was written while he was down and out in Dublin and the much later *Pomes Penyeach* was published partly to show critics that the writer of *Finnegans Wake* was not completely off his head. All his poems have been published in the one collection *Poems and Epiphanies*.

Most of the sayings in this collection come from Joyce's novels and short stories. Other works are *Giacomo Joyce*, a series of prose sketches, his one play *Exiles*, and various lectures and essays brought together in *The Critical Writings of James Joyce*. Some of the sayings have been recorded by people who conversed with him and subsequently either wrote their own accounts or were interviewed for their memories. A notable but not unsurprising exception is Samuel Beckett; they knew each other for many years in Paris and they remained good friends. It was Beckett with whom Joyce's daughter Lucia became infatuated, but the young Irish writer was unable to reciprocate.

Recommended reading for anyone who wants to know more about Joyce's life is Brenda Maddox's biography of Nora Barnacle, a book which complements Richard Ellmann's more reverential biography of James Joyce himself.

Primary sources

The Critical Writings of James Joyce (London: Faber, 1959)
Dubliners (1914)
Exiles (New York: The Viking Press, 1951)
Finnegans Wake (1939)
Giacomo Joyce (London: Faber, 1968)
Poems and Epiphanies (London: Faber, 1990)
A Portrait of the Artist as a Young Man (1914-15)
Stephen Hero (New York: New Directions, 1963)
Ulysses (1922)
Letters of James Joyce, ed. Stuart Gilbert (London: Faber, 1957)
Letters of James Joyce, vols. II & III, ed. Richard Ellmann
    (London: Faber, 1966)

Secondary sources

Conversations with James Joyce, Arthur Power (London: 1974)
Dublin's Joyce, Hugh Kenner (New York: Columbia University
    Press, 1956)
James Joyce, Richard Ellmann (Oxford: 1982)
James Joyce and the Making of 'Ulysses' & other writings, Frank
    Budgen (Oxford: 1972)
My Brother's Keeper: James Joyce's Early Years, Stanislaus Joyce
    (New York: The Viking Press, 1958)
Nora: A Biography of Nora Joyce, Brenda Maddox (London:
    Hamish Hamilton, 1988)
Our Friend James Joyce, Mary and Padraic Colum (New York:
    1958)

Growing Up

I stand, the self-doomed, unafraid,
Unfellowed, friendless and alone,
Indifferent as the herring-bone,
Firm as the mountain-ridges where
I flash my antlers on the air.

Poems and Epiphanies, 'The Holy Office'

He, at least, though living at the farthest remove from the
centre of European culture, marooned on an island in the
ocean, though inheriting a will broken by doubt ... would lead
his own life according to what he recognised as the voice of a
new humanity, active, unafraid and unashamed.

Stephen Hero, p. 194

Once upon a time and a very good time it was there was a
moocow coming down along the road and this moocow that
was down along the road met a nicens little boy named baby
tuckoo.

A Portrait of the Artist as a Young Man, ch. 1

The Vances lived in number seven. They had a different father
and mother. They were Eileen's father and mother. When they
were grown up he was going to marry Eileen.

ib.

He hid under the table. His mother said:
– O, Stephen will apologise.
Dante said:
– O, if not, the eagles will come and pull out his eyes.
Pull out his eyes,
Apologise
Apologise,
Pull out his eyes.

ib.

Stephen Dedalus is my name,
Ireland is my nation.
Clongowes is my dwellingplace
And heaven my expectation.

ib.

God was God's name just as his name was Stephen. *Dieu* was the French for God and that was God's name too; and when anyone prayed to God and said *Dieu* then God knew at once that it was a French person that was praying.

ib.

– Poor Parnell! he cried loudly. My dead king!
He sobbed loudly and bitterly.
Stephen, raising his terrorstricken face, saw that his father's eyes were full of tears.

ib.

A hot burning stinging tingling blow like the loud crack of a broken stick made his trembling hand crumple together like a leaf in the fire: and at the sound and the pain scalding tears were driven into his eyes.

ib.

A cry sprang to his lips, a prayer to be let off. But though the tears scalded his eyes and his limbs quivered with pain and fright he held back the hot tears and the cry that scalded his throat.
– Other hand! shouted the prefect of studies.

ib.

An image of himself, grown older and sadder, standing in a moonlit garden with Mercedes who had so many years before slighted his love, and with a sadly proud gesture of refusal, saying:
– Madam, I never eat muscatel grapes.

ib. ch. 2

He wanted to meet in the real world the unsubstantial image which his soul so constantly beheld.

ib.

– This is horse piss and rotted straw, he thought. It is a good odour to breathe. It will calm my heart. My heart is quiet calm now. I will go back.

ib.

It shocked him to find in the outer world a trace of what he had deemed till then a brutish and individual malady of his own mind.

ib.

Stephen watched the three glasses being raised from the
counter as his father and his two cronies drank to the memory
of their past. An abyss of fortune or of temperament sundered
him from them. His mind seemed older than theirs: it shone
coldly on their strifes and happiness and regrets like a moon
upon a younger earth.

ib.

Nothing stirred within his soul but a cold and cruel and
loveless lust. His childhood was dead or lost and with it his
soul capable of simple joys and he was drifting amid life like
the barren shell of the moon.

ib.

A figure that had seemed to him by day demure and innocent
came towards him by night through the winding darkness of
sleep, her face transfigured by a lecherous cunning, her eyes
bright with brutish joy.

ib.

His sins trickled from his lips, one by one, trickled in shameful
drops from his soul festering and oozing like a sore, a squalid
stream of vice. The last sins oozed forth, sluggish, filthy. There
was no more to tell. He bowed his head, overcome.
The priest was silent.

ib. ch. 3

To merge his life in the common tide of other lives was harder
for him than any fasting or prayer, and it was his constant
failure to do this to his own satisfaction which caused in his
soul a sensation of spiritual dryness together with a growth of
doubts and scruples.

ib. ch. 4

His actual reception of the eucharist did not bring him the
same dissolving moments of virginal selfsurrender as did those
spiritual communions made by him sometimes at the close of
some visit to the Blessed Sacrament.

ib.

He smiled to think that it was this disorder, the misrule and
confusion of his father's house ... which was to win the day in
his soul.

ib.

His cheeks were aflame; his body was aglow; his limbs were trembling. On and on and on and on he strode, far out over the sands, singing wildly to the sea, crying to greet the advent of the life that had cried to him.

ib.

A wild angel had appeared to him, the angel of mortal youth and beauty, an envoy from the fair courts of life, to throw open before him in an instant of ecstasy the gates of all the ways of error and glory. On and on and on and on!

ib.

A sense of fear of the unknown moved in the heart of his weariness, a fear of symbols and portents, of the hawklike man whose name he bore soaring out of his captivity on osierwoven wings.

ib. ch. 5

But yet it wounded him to think that he would never be but a shy guest at the feast of the world's culture and that the monkish learning, in terms of which he was striving to forge out an aesthetic philosophy, was held no higher by the age he lived in than the subtle and curious jargons of heraldry and falconry.

ib.

– It is a curious thing, do you know, Cranly said dispassionately, how your mind is supersaturated with the religion in which you say you disbelieve.

ib.

I will not serve that in which I no longer believe, whether it call itself my home, my fatherland or my church.

ib.

I will try to express myself in some mode of life or art as freely as I can and as wholly as I can, using for my defence the only arms I allow myself to use – silence, exile and cunning.

ib.

Asked me was it true I was going away and why. Told him the shortest way to Tara was *via* Holyhead.

ib.

Talked rapidly of myself and my plans. In the midst of it
unluckily I made a sudden gesture of a revolutionary nature. I
must have looked like a fellow throwing a handful of peas up
into the air. People began to look at us. She shook hands a
moment after and, in going away, said she hoped I would do
what I said.

 Now I call that friendly, don't you?

ib.

Mother is putting away my new secondhand clothes in order.
She prays now, she says, that I may learn in my own life and
away from home and friends what the heart is and what it
feels. Amen. So be it.

ib.

Old father, old artificer, stand me now and ever in good stead.
ib.

You wouldn't kneel down to pray for your mother on her
deathbed when she asked you. Why? Because you have the
cursed jesuit strain in you, only it's injected the wrong way.
Ulysses, Episode 1

History, Stephen said, is a nightmare from which I am trying to
awake.

ib., Episode 2

You told the Clongowes gentry you had an uncle a judge and
an uncle a general in the army. Come out of them, Stephen.
Beauty is not there.

ib., Episode 3

You prayed to the Blessed Virgin that you might not have a red
nose. You prayed to the devil in Serpentine avenue that the
fubsy widow in front might lift her clothes still more from the
wet street.

ib.

Reading two pages apiece of seven books every night, eh? I
was young. You bowed to yourself in the mirror, stepping
forward to applause earnestly, striking face.

ib.

The sentimentalist is he who would enjoy without incurring
the immense debtorship for a thing done. *Signed Dedalus.*
ib., Episode 9

A man of genius makes no mistakes. His errors are volitional and are the portals of discovery.   *ib.*

The son unborn mars beauty: born, he brings pain, divides affection, increases care. He is a new male: his growth is his father's decline, his youth his father's envy, his friend his father's enemy.   *ib.*

Fabulous artificer. The hawklike man. You flew. Whereto? Newhaven-Dieppe, steerage passenger. Paris and back.

ib.

There's a saying of Goethe's which Mr Magee likes to quote. Beware of what you wish for in youth because you will get it in middle life.   *ib.*

He winged away on a wildgoup's chase across the kathartic ocean and made synthetic ink and sensitive paper for his own end out of his wit's waste.

Finnegans Wake, p. 185

You were bred, fed, fostered and fattened from holy childhood up in this two easter island on the piejaw of hilarious heaven and roaring the other place   *ib.*, p. 188

Hidden and discovered, nay, condemned fool, anarch, egoarch, hieresiarch, you have reared your disunited kingdom on the vacuum of your own most intensely doubtful soul.

ib.

He's weird, I tell you, and middayevil down to his vegetable soul. Never mind his falls feet and his tanbark complexion. That's why he was forbidden tomate and was warmed off the ricecourse of marrimoney.   *ib.*, p. 423

My leaves have drifted from me. All. But one clings still. I'll bear it on me. To remind me of. Lff! So soft this morning, ours. Yes. Carry me along, taddy, like you done through the toy fair!

ib., p. 628

I may be blind. I looked for a long time at a head of reddish brown hair and decided it was not yours. I went home quite dejected. I would like to make an appointment but it might not suit you. I hope you will be kind enough to make one with me – if you have not forgotten me!   *Letter*, 15 June 1904

People

A child is sleeping:
An old man gone.
O father forsaken,
Forgive your son!

Pomes Penyeach, 'Ecce Puer'

Wherever thou [Nora Barnacle] art shall be Erin to me.
Poems and Epiphanies, 'Alphabetical Notebook',
entry under 'Nora'

Rapid motion through space elates one; so does notoriety; so does the possession of money. These were three good reasons for Jimmy's excitement.

Dubliners, 'After the Race'

His head was large, globular and oily; it sweated in all weathers; and his large round hat, set upon it sideways, looked like a bulb which had grown out of another.

ib., 'Two Gallants'

He spoke roughly in order to belie his air of gentility for his entry had been followed by a pause of talk. His face was heated. To appear natural he pushed his cap back on his head and planted his elbows on the table. The mechanic and the two work-girls examined him point by point before resuming their conversation in a subdued voice.

ib.

– Can't you tell us? he said. Did you try her?
Corley halted at the first lamp and stared grimly before him. Then with a grave gesture he extended a hand towards the light and, smiling, opened it slowly to the gaze of his disciple. A small gold coin shone in his palm.

ib.

She dealt with moral problems as a cleaver deals with meat: and in this case she had made up her mind.

ib., 'The Boarding House'

Mr Duffy abhorred anything which betokened physical or mental disorder. A medieval doctor would have called him saturnine.

ib., 'A Painful Case'

He lived at a little distance from his body, regarding his own acts with doubtful self-glances.

ib.

He had an odd autobiographical habit which led him to compose in his mind from time to time a short sentence about himself containing a subject in the third person and a predicate in the past tense.

ib.

Their gaze began with a defiant note but was confused by what seemed a deliberate swoon of the pupil into the iris, revealing for an instant a temperament of great sensibility. The pupil reasserted itself quickly, this half-disclosed nature fell again under the reign of prudence, and her astrakhan jacket, moulding a bosom of a certain fullness, struck the note of defiance more definitely.

ib.

He thought that in her eyes he would ascend to an angelical stature; and, as he attached the fervent nature of his companion more and more closely to him, he heard the strange impersonal voice which he recognised as his own, insisting on the soul's incurable loneliness.

ib.

He stood still to listen. Why had he withheld life from her? Why had he sentenced her to death? He felt his moral nature falling to pieces.

ib.

He opened his very long mouth suddenly to express disappointment and at the same time opened wide his very bright blue eyes to express pleasure and surprise.

ib., 'Ivy Day in the Committee Room'

Mr. Crofton said that it was a very fine piece of writing.

ib.

She respected her husband in the same way as she respected
the General Post Office, as something large, secure and fixed;
and though she knew the small number of his talents she
appreciated his abstract value as a male.

ib., 'A Mother'

If you want a thing well done and no flies about, you go to a
Jesuit. They're the boyos have influence.

ib., 'Grace'

The men that is now is only all palaver and what they can get
out of you.

ib., 'The Dead'

Though she was stout in build and stood erect her slow eyes
and parted lips gave her the appearance of a woman who did
not know where she was or where she was going.

ib.

Aunt Julia was more vivacious. Her face, healthier than her
sister's, was all puckers and creases, like a shrivelled red apple,
and her hair, braided in the same old-fashioned way, had not
lost its ripe nut colour.

ib.

Freddy Malins exploded, before he had well reached the
climax of his story, in a kink of high-pitched bronchitic
laughter and, setting down his untasted and overflowing glass,
began to rub the knuckles of his left fist backwards and
forwards into his left eye, repeating words of his last phrase as
well as his fit of laughter would allow him.

ib.

But we are living in a sceptical and, if I may use the phrase, a
thought-tormented age: and sometimes I fear that this new
generation, educated or hypereducated as it is, will lack those
qualities of humanity, of hospitality, of kindly humour which
belonged to an older day.

ib.

He saw himself as a ludicrous figure, acting as a pennyboy for
his aunts, a nervous well-meaning sentimentalist, orating to
vulgarians and idealising his own clownish lusts, the pitiable
fatuous fellow he had caught a glimpse of in the mirror.

ib.

Stephen began to enumerate glibly his father's attributes.
– A medical student, an oarsman, a tenor, an amateur actor, a
shouting politician, a small landlord, a small investor, a
drinker, a good fellow, a storyteller, somebody's secretary,
something in a distillery, a taxgatherer, a bankrupt and at
present a praiser of his own past.

A Portrait of the Artist as a Young Man, ch. 5

When I makes tea I makes tea, as old mother Grogan said. And
when I makes water I makes water.

Ulysses, Episode 1

An elderly man shot up near the spur of rock a blowing red
face. He scrambled up by the stones, water glistening on his
pate and on its garland of grey hair, water rilling over his chest
and paunch and spilling jets out of his black sagging loincloth.

ib.

– Man delights him [Shakespeare] not nor woman neither,
Stephen said. He returns after a life of absence to that spot of
earth where he was born, where he has always been, man and
boy, a silent witness and there, his journey of life ended, he
plants his mulberrytree in the earth. Then dies.

ib., Episode 9

Enchainted, dear sweet Stainusless, young confessor, dearer
dearest, we herehear, aboutobloss, Ó coelicola, thee salutamt.

Finnegans Wake, p. 237

Sam [Samuel Beckett] knows miles bettern me how to work the
miracle ... He'll prisckly soon hand tune your Erin's ear for
you.

ib., p. 467

And it's old and old it's sad and old it's sad and weary I go
back to you, my cold father, my cold mad father, my cold mad
feary father

ib., p. 627

When I looked on her face [his mother] as she lay in her coffin
– a face grey and wasted with cancer – I understood that I was
looking on the face of a victim and I cursed the system which
had made her a victim

Letter, 29 August 1904

People live together in the same houses all their lives and at the end they are as far apart as ever.

Letter, 16 September 1904

The more I hear of the political, philosophical, ethical zeal and labours of the brilliant members of [Ezra] Pound's big brass band, the more I wonder why I was ever let into it.

Letter, 22 November 1929

My father had an extraordinary affection for me. He was the silliest man I ever knew and yet cruelly shrewd. He thought and talked of me up to his last breath. I was very fond of him, always, being a sinner myself, and even liked his faults. Hundreds of pages and scores of characters in my books came from him.

Letter, 17 January 1932

He seems to have read *Ulysses* from first to last without one smile. The only thing to do in such a case is to change one's drink.

Letter, 22 October 1932

She'll [Lucia Joyce] get all right they say. One needs all Job's patience with Solomon's wisdom and the Queen of Sheba's pinmoney thrown in.

Letter, 25 April 1934

Haven't time to read it [Samuel Beckett's *More Pricks Than Kicks*]. But looked at it here and there before quitting Paris. He has talent, I think.

Letter, 9 August 1934

The only decent people I ever saw at a race course were the horses.

Letter, 20 December 1934

They did not throw him [Charles Stuart Parnell] to the English wolves; they tore him to pieces themselves.

Critical Writings, p. 228

The Greeks have always brought me good luck.

Quoted in M. & P. Colum, *Our Friend James Joyce*

We have met too late. You [W.B. Yeats] are too old for me to have any effect on you.

> Quoted in R. Ellmann, *James Joyce*, ch. 7

You know people never value anything unless they have to steal it. Even an alley cat would rather shake an old bone out of the garbage than come up and eat a nicely prepared chop from your saucer.

> *ib.*, ch. 29

Paul Léon tells me that when I stand bent over at a street corner I look like a questionmark.

> *ib.*, ch. 34

I don't love anyone except my family.

> *ib.*, ch. 35

Who is Sylvia [Beach], what is she
That all our scribes commend her?
Yankee, young and brave is she
The West this grace did lend her
That all books might published be

> Quoted in B. Maddox, *Nora*, ch. 10

How full of grace and invention is Mozart after the muscle-bound Beethoven.

> Quoted in F. Budgen, *James Joyce and the Making of 'Ulysses'*

My own idea [of the thoughts of Penelope in a photograph of the sculptured woman] is that she is trying to recollect what Ulysses looks like. You see, he has been away many years, and they had no photographs in those days.

> *ib.*

Ireland

This lovely land that always sent
Her writers and artists to banishment
And in a spirit of Irish fun
Betrayed her own leaders, one by one.

Poems and Epiphanies, 'Gas from a Burner'

Oh Ireland my first and only love
Where Christ and Caesar are hand in glove!   *ib.*

At the crest of the hill at Inchicore sightseers had gathered in
clumps to watch the cars careering homeward and through
this channel of poverty and inaction the Continent sped its
wealth and industry. Now and again the clumps of people
raised the cheer of the gratefully oppressed.

Dubliners, 'After the Race'

– And haven't you your language to keep in touch with – Irish?
asked Miss Ivors
– Well, said Gabriel, if it comes to that, you know, Irish is not
my language.   *ib.,* 'The Dead'

Yes, the newspapers were right: snow was general all over
Ireland. It was falling on every part of the dark central plain,
on the treeless hills, falling softly upon the Bog of Allen and,
further westwards, softly falling into the dark mutinous
Shannon waves.   *ib.*

The peasant women stood at the halfdoors, the men stood here
and there. The lovely smell there was in the wintry air: the
smell of Clane: rain and wintry air and turf smouldering and
corduroy.   *A Portrait of the Artist as a Young Man,* ch. 1

The grey block of Trinity on his left, set heavily in the city's
ignorance like a dull stone set in a cumbrous ring.

ib., ch. 5

– My ancestors threw off their language and took another,
Stephen said. They allowed a handful of foreigners to subject
them. Do you fancy I am going to pay in my own life and
person debts they made?   *ib.*

– When you make the next rebellion with hurleysticks, said Stephen, and want the indispensable informer, tell me. I can find you a few in this college.   *ib.*

– No honourable and sincere man, said Stephen, has given up to you his life and his youth and his affections from the days of Tone to those of Parnell, but you sold him to the enemy or failed him in need or reviled him and left him for another.

ib.

Ireland is the old sow that eats her farrow.   *ib.*

When the soul of a man is born in this country there are nets flung at it to hold it back from flight. You talk to me of nationality, language, religion. I shall try to fly by those nets.

ib.

He stared angrily back at the softly lit drawingrooms of the hotel in which he imagined the sleek lives of the patricians of Ireland housed in calm. They thought of army commissions and land agents: peasants greeted them along the roads in the country.   *ib.*

How could he hit their conscience or how cast his shadow over the imaginations of their daughters, before their squires begat upon them, that they might breed a race less ignoble than their own.   *ib.*

RICHARD: There are those who left her to seek the bread by which men live and there are others, nay, her most favoured children, who left her to seek in other lands that food of the spirit by which a nation of human beings is sustained in life.

Exiles, Act 3

– It is a symbol of Irish art. The cracked lookingglass of a servant.   *Ulysses*, Episode 1

We feel in England that we have treated you rather unfairly. It seems history is to blame.   *ib.*

Of lost leaders, the betrayed, wild escapes. Disguises, clutched at, gone, not here.   *ib.*, Episode 3

[A] good puzzle would be [to] cross Dublin without passing a pub.   *ib.*, Episode 4

– We can't change the country. Let us change the subject.
ib., Episode 16

riverrun, past Eve and Adam's, from swerve of shore to bend
of bay, brings us by a commodius vicus of recirculation back to
Howth Castle and Environs. *Finnegans Wake*, p. 3

So this is Dyoublong?
Hush! Caution! Echoland! *ib.*, p. 13

The wastobe land, a lottuse land, a luctuous land,
Emerald-illium. *ib.*, p. 62

He even ran away with hunself and became a farsoonerite,
saying he would far sooner muddle through the hash of lentils
in Europe than meddle with Irrland's split little pea.
ib., p. 171

Ireland sober is Ireland stiff. *ib.*, p. 214

From time to time I see in publishers' lists announcements of
books on Irish subjects, so that I think people might be willing
to pay for the special odour of corruption which, I hope, floats
over my stories. *Letter*, 16 October 1905

My intention was to write a chapter in the moral history of my
country and I chose Dublin for the scene because that city
seemed to me the centre of paralysis.
Letter, 5 May 1906

What I object to most of all in his paper [an attack on the
English for their sexual habits] is that it is educating the people
of Ireland on the old pap of racial hatred whereas anyone can
see that if the Irish question exists, it exists for the Irish
proletariat chiefly. *Letter*, 25 September 1906

Sometimes thinking of Ireland it seems to me that I have been
unnecessarily harsh. I have reproduced (in *Dubliners* at least)
none of the attractions of the city for I have never felt at my
ease in any city since I left it except in Paris.
ib.

How sick sick, sick I am of Dublin! It is the city of failure, of
rancour and of unhappiness. I long to be out of it.
Letter, 22 August 1909

The soul of the country is weakened by centuries of useless struggles and broken treaties, and individual initiative is paralysed by the influence and admonitions of the church.

Critical Writings, pp. 171-2

No one who has any self-respect stays in Ireland, but flees afar as though from a country that has undergone the visitation of an angered Jove. *ib.*

The old men, the corrupt, the children, and the poor stay at home, where the double yoke wears another groove in the tamed neck; and around the death bed, where the poor anaemic, almost lifeless body lies in agony, the rulers give orders and the priests administer last rites.

ib.

It is well past time for Ireland to have done once and for all with failure.

ib., p. 174

She has betrayed her heroes, always in the hour of need and always without gaining recompense. She has hounded her spiritual creators into exile only to boast about them.

ib., 'The Home Rule Comet'

She has served only one master well, the Roman Catholic Church, which, however, is accustomed to pay its faithful in long term drafts. *ib.*

All Irish whiskies use the water of the Liffey; all but one filter it, but John Jameson's uses it mud and all. That gives it its special quality.

Quoted in R. Ellmann, *James Joyce*

I want to give a picture of Dublin so complete that if the city one day suddenly disappeared from the earth it could be reconstructed out of my book [*Ulysses*].

Quoted in F. Budgen, *James Joyce and the Making of 'Ulysses'*

Everybody [in Dublin] has time to hail a friend and start a conversation about a third party, Pat, Barney or Tim. 'Have you seen Barney lately? Is he still off the drink?' 'Ay, sure he is. I was with him last night and he drank nothing but claret.'

ib.

Women

My words in her mind: cold polished stones sinking through a quagmire.

Giacomo Joyce

As she mused the pitiful vision of her mother's life laid its spell on the very quick of her being – that life of commonplace sacrifices closing in final craziness.

Dubliners, 'Eveline'

She set her white face to him, passive, like a helpless animal. Her eyes gave him no sign of love or farewell or recognition.

ib.

He asked himself what is a woman standing on the stairs in the shadow, listening to distant music, a symbol of.

ib., 'The Dead'

It had shocked him, too, when he had felt for the first time beneath his trembling fingers the brittle texture of a woman's stocking for ... it was only amid softworded phrases or within rosesoft stuffs that he had dared to conceive of the soul or body of a woman moving with tender life.

A Portrait of the Artist as a Young Man, ch. 4

And if he had judged her harshly? If her life were a simple rosary of hours, her life simple and strange as a bird's life, gay in the morning, restless all day, tired at sundown? Her life simple and wilful as a bird's heart?

ib., ch. 5

He had told himself bitterly as he walked through the streets that she was a figure of the womanhood of her country, a batlike soul waking to the consciousness of itself in darkness and secrecy and loneliness, tarrying awhile, loveless and sinless, with her mild lover and leaving him to whisper of innocent transgressions in the latticed ear of a priest.

ib.

Women all for caste till you touch the spot. Handsome is and handsome does. Reserved about to yield.

Ulysses, Episode 5

The waxen pallor of her face was almost spiritual in its ivorylike purity though her rosebud mouth was a genuine Cupid's bow, Greekly perfect.

ib., Episode 13

she had too much old chat in her about politics and earthquakes and the end of the world let us have a bit of fun first God help the world if all the women were her sort down on bathingsuits and lownecks of course nobody wanted her to wear them I suppose she was pious because no man would look at her twice

ib., Episode 18

curious the way its made 2 the same in case of twins theyre supposed to represent beauty placed up there like those statues in the museum one of them pretending to hide it with her hand are they so beautiful of course compared with what a man looks like with his two bags full and his other thing hanging down out of him or sticking up at you like a hatrack no wonder they hide it with a cabbageleaf

ib.

and they always want to see a stain on the bed to know youre a virgin for them thats all thats troubling them theyre such fools too you could be a widow or divorced 40 times over a daub of red ink would do or blackberry juice

ib.

I dont care what anybody says itd be much better for the world to be governed by the women in it you wouldnt see women going and killing one another and slaughtering

ib.

... the vaulting feminine libido of those interbranching ogham sex upandinsweeps sternly controlled and easily repersuaded by the uniform matteroffactness of a meandering male fist.

Finnegans Wake, p. 123

O tell me all about Anna Livia! I want to hear all about Anna Livia. Well, you know Anna Livia? Yes, of course we all know Anna Livia. Tell me all. Tell me now. You'll die when you hear.

ib., p. 196

she is so pretty, truth to tell, wildwood's eyes and primarose
hair, quietly, all the woods so wild, in mauves of moss and
daphnedews, how all so still she lay, neath of the whitethorn,
child of tree, like some losthappy leaf, like blowing flower
stilled

ib., p. 556

All me life I have been lived among them [men] but now they
are becoming lothed to me. And I am lothing their little warm
tricks. And lothing their mean cosy turns. And all the greedy
gushes out through their small souls.

ib., p. 627

Do you notice how women when they write disregard stops
and capital letters?

Letter, 9 October 1906

No man, I believe, can ever be worthy of a woman's love.

Letter, 19 August 1909

When I find a lady who is content with her own picture I will
send a bouquet to the Pope.

Letter, 3 June 1935

Do you know how to tell whether a woman is any good or not?
Well, take her to a picture gallery, and explain the pictures to
her. If she breaks wind, she's all right.

Quoted in R. Ellmann, *James Joyce,* ch. 26

He [Jesus] was a bachelor and never lived with a woman.
Surely living with a woman is one of the most difficult things a
man has to do, and he never did it.

Quoted in F. Budgen, *James Joyce and the Making of 'Ulysses'*

Literature

But all these men of whom I speak
Make me the sewer of their clique.
That they may dream their dreamy dreams
I carry off their filthy streams

Poems and Epiphanies, 'The Holy Office'

By an epiphany he meant a sudden spiritual manifestation,
whether in the vulgarity of speech or of gesture or in a
memorable phase of the mind itself.   *Stephen Hero*

Then all at once I see it and I know at once what it is: epiphany.
– What?
– Imagine my glimpses at that clock as the gropings of a
spiritual eye which seeks to adjust its vision to an exact focus.
The moment the focus is reached the object is epiphanized.

ib.

a hawklike man flying sunwards above the sea, a prophecy of
the end he had been born to serve and had been following
through the mists of childhood and boyhood, a symbol of the
artist forging anew in his workshop out of the sluggish matter
of the earth a new soaring impalpable imperishable being?

A Portrait of the Artist as a Young Man, ch. 4

The artist, like the God of the creation, remains within or
behind or beyond or above his handiwork, invisible, refined
out of existence, indifferent, paring his fingernails.

ib., ch. 5

The radiance of which he [Aquinas] speaks is the scholastic
quidditas, the *whatness* of a thing. This supreme quality is felt
by the artist when the aesthetic image is first conceived in his
imagination.

ib.

The flag is up on the playhouse by the bankside. The bear
Sackerson growls in the pit near it, Paris garden.
Canvasclimbers who sailed with Drake chew their sausages
among the groundlings.

Ulysses, Episode 3

– Upon my word it makes my blood boil to hear anyone
compare Aristotle with Plato.
– Which of the two, Stephen asked, would have banished me
from his commonwealth?   *ib.*, Episode 9

No, so holp me Petault, it is not a miseffectual whyacinthinous
riot of blots and blurs and bars and balls and hoops and
wriggles and juxtaposed jottings linked by spurts of speed: it
only looks as like as damn it

Finnegans Wake, p. 118

sentenced to be nuzzled over a full trillion times for ever and a
night till his noodle sink or swim by that ideal reader suffering
from an ideal insomnia

ib., p. 120

maid the inspissated grime of his glaucous den making believe
to read his usylessly unreadable Blue Book of Eccles

ib., p. 179

if one has the stomach to add the breakages, upheavals,
distortions, inversions of all this chambermade music one
stands, given a grain of goodwill, a fair chance of actually
seeing the whirling dervish, Tumult, son of Thunder, self
exiled in upon his ego

ib., p. 184

wrote over every square inch of the only foolscap available, his
own body, till by its corrosive sublimation one continuous
present tense integument slowly unfolded

ib., p. 186

When you remember that Dublin has been a capital for
thousands of years, that it is the 'second' city of the British
Empire, that it is nearly three times as big as Venice it seems
strange that no artist has given it to the world.

Letter, 24 September 1905

I have written it [*Dubliners*] for the most part in a style of
scrupulous meanness … I cannot alter what I have written.

Letter, 5 May 1906

I have come to the conclusion that I cannot write without
offending people.

ib.

It is not my fault that the odour of ashpits and old weeds and offal hangs round my stories. I seriously believe that you will retard the course of civilisation in Ireland by preventing the Irish people from having one good look at themselves in my nicely polished looking glass.

Letter, 23 June 1906

It [*Ulysses*] cost me nine years of my life. I was in correspondence with seven solicitors, one hundred and twenty newspapers, and several men of letters about it – all of whom, except Mr Ezra Pound, refused to aid me.

Letter, 8 July 1917

The task I set myself technically in writing a book from eighteen different points of view and in as many styles, all apparently unknown or undiscovered by my fellow tradesmen, that and the nature of the legend chosen would be enough to upset anyone's mental balance.

Letter, 24 June 1921

What the language will look like when I have finished [*Finnegans Wake*] I don't know. But having declared war I shall go on *jusqu'au bout*.

Letter, 11 November 1925

Another (or rather many) says he is imitating Lewis Carroll. I never read him till Mrs Nutting gave me a book ... But then I never read Rabelais either though nobody will believe this.

Letter, 31 May 1927

Perhaps it [*Finnegans Wake*] is insanity. One will be able to judge in a century.

Letter, January 1928

Publishers and printers alike seemed to agree among themselves, no matter how divergent their points of view were in other matters, not to publish anything of mine as I wrote it.

Letter, 2 April 1932

No less than twenty-two publishers and printers read the manuscript of *Dubliners* and when at last it was printed some very kind person bought out the entire edition and had it burnt in Dublin.

ib.

I do not know where the British and American papers get their scare headlines about me. I have never given an interview in my life and do not receive journalists. Nor do I understand why they should consider an unread writer as good copy.

Letter, 10 November 1932

Incidentally you will discover the title of the book [*Finnegans Wake*] which my wife has kept secret for seventeen years, being the only one who knew it. I think I can see some lofty thinkers and noble livers turning away from it with a look of pained displeasure.   *Letter*, 28 January 1939

I don't know why they [Marxist critics] attack me. Nobody in any of my books is worth more than a thousand pounds.

Quoted in R. Ellmann, *James Joyce*, Introduction

The demand that I make of my reader is that he should devote his whole life to reading my works.   *ib.*, ch. 16

Ulysses didn't want to go off to Troy; he knew that the official reason for the war, the dissemination of the culture of Hellas, was only a pretext for the Greek merchants, who were seeking new markets. When the recruiting officers arrived, he happened to be ploughing. He pretended to be mad. Thereupon they placed his little two-year-old son in the furrow. Observe the beauty of the motifs: the only man in Hellas who is against the war, and the father.

ib., ch. 25

I've put in [*Ulysses*] so many enigmas and puzzles that it will keep the professors busy for centuries arguing over what I meant, and that's the only way of insuring one's immortality.

ib., ch. 30

The pity is the public will demand and find a moral in my book [*Ulysses*], or worse they may take it in some serious way, and on the honour of a gentleman, there is not one single serious word in it.   *ib.*

It [*The Book of Kells*] is the most purely Irish thing we have, and some of the big initial letters which swing right across the page have an essential quality of a chapter of *Ulysses*. Indeed, you can compare much of my work to the intricate illuminations.

ib., ch. 31

If *Ulysses* isn't fit to read, life isn't fit to live.   *ib.*

Yes. Some of the means I use [in *Finnegans Wake*] are trivial –
and some are quadrivial.

ib.

If anyone doesn't understand a passage, all he need do is read
it aloud.   *ib.*, ch. 33

My art is not a mirror held up to nature. Nature mirrors my art.
ib., ch. 35

The most natural thing for a writer to do is to call a spade a
spade. The mistake which some moralists make, even today, is
that they hate unpleasant phenomena less than they do those
who record them.

ib., ch. 36

I am James Joyce. I understand that you are to translate
Ulysses, and I have come from Paris to tell you not to alter a
single word.   *ib.*

For God's sake don't talk politics. I'm not interested in politics.
The only thing that interests me is style.

ib.

Why should I write anything else? Nobody reads this book
[*Finnegans Wake*].

ib., ch. 37

I haven't let this young man [Stephen Dedalus] off very lightly,
have I? Many writers have written about themselves. I wonder
if any one of them has been as candid as I have?
Quoted in F. Budgen, *James Joyce and the Making of 'Ulysses'*

I have just got a letter asking me why I don't give Bloom a rest.
The writer of it wants more Stephen. But Stephen no longer
interests me to the same extent. He has a shape that can't be
changed.

ib.

There's only one kind of critic I do resent … The kind that
affects to believe that I am writing with my tongue in my
cheek.

ib.

It [*Ulysses*] is the work of a sceptic, but I don't want it to appear the work of a cynic. I don't want to hurt or offend those of my countrymen who are devoting their lives to a cause [nationalism] they feel to be necessary and just.

ib.

I should hesitate [choosing one book for a desert island] between Dante and Shakespeare but not for long. The Englishman is richer and would get my vote.

ib.

I am inclined to think that Balzac's reputation rests on a lot of neat generalisations about life.

ib.

Rousseau, confessing to stealing silver spoons he had really stolen, is much more interesting than one of Dostoevsky's people confessing to an unreal murder.

ib.

Strange that it should have been left to an Irishman [George Moore's *Ester Waters*] to write the best novel of modern English life!

ib.

Of all English writers Chaucer is the clearest. He is as precise and slick as a Frenchman.

ib.

Naustikaa [episode 13 of *Ulysses*] is written in a namby-pamby jammy marmalady drawersy (alto là) style.

ib.

The companions of Ulysses disobey the commands of Pallas. They slay and flay the oxen of the Sungod and all are drowned save the prudent and pious Ulysses. I interpret the killing of the sacred oxen as the crime against fecundity by sterilising the act of coition. *ib.*

I am writing *Ithaca* [episode 17 of *Ulysses*] in the form of a mathematical catechism. All events are resolved into their cosmic physical, psychical etc. equivalents … Bloom and Stephen therby become heavenly bodies, wanderers like the stars at which they gaze.

ib.

There is an atmosphere of spiritual effort here [Paris]. No other city is quite like it. It is a racecourse tension. I wake early, often at five o'clock, and start writing at once.

ib.

Don't you think there is a certain resemblance between the mystery of the Mass and what I am trying to do? I mean that I am trying ... to give people some kind of intellectual pleasure or spiritual enjoyment by converting the bread of everyday life into something that has a permanent artistic life of its own.

Quoted in S. Joyce, *My Brother's Keeper*

Your wife said what I read [*Finnegans Wake*] was outside literature. Tell her it may be outside literature now, but its future is inside literature.

Quoted in M. & P. Colum, *Our Friend James Joyce*

In the Paris jungle, stampede of omnibuses and trumpeting of taxielephants etc and in this caravanserai peopled by American loudspeakers I compose ridiculous prose writing on a green suitcase which I bought in Bognor.

Quoted in H. Kenner, *Dublin's Joyce*

I felt so completely exhausted [after finishing *Finnegans Wake*] as if all the blood had run out of my brain. I sat for a long while on a street bench, unable to move.

ib.

The purpose of *The Doll's House*, for instance, was the emancipation of women, which has caused the greatest revolution in our time in the most important relationship there is – that between men and women; the revolt of women against the idea that they are the mere instruments of men.

Quoted in A. Power, *Conversations with James Joyce*, p. 35

Pub Talk

The man drank it at a gulp and asked for a caraway seed. He put his penny on the counter and, leaving the curate to grope for it in the gloom, retreated out of the snug as furtively as he had entered it.

Dubliners, 'Counterparts'

So I just looked at him – coolly, you know, and looked at her. Then I looked back at him again – taking my time, you know. *I don't think that's a fair question to put to me*, say I.

Nosey Flynn was sitting up in his usual corner of Davy Byrne's and, when he heard the story, he stood Farrington a half-one, saying it was as smart a thing as ever he heard. Farrington stood a drink in his turn.

ib.

He had a brave manner of coming up to a party of them in a bar and holding himself nimbly at the borders of the company until he was included in a round. He was a sporting vagrant armed with a vast stock of stories, limericks and riddles.

ib., 'Two Gallants'

– No, by God! asserted Mr Dedalus. I'll sing a tenor song against him or I'll vault a fivebarred gate against him or I'll run with him after the hounds across the country as I did thirty years ago.

A Portrait of the Artist as a Young Man, ch. 2

– And thanks be to God, Johnny, said Mr Dedalus, that we lived so long and did so little harm.
– But did so much good, Simon said the little man gravely. Thanks be to God we lived so long and did so much good.

ib.

Smells of men. Spaton sawdust, sweetish warmish cigarettesmoke, reek of plug, spilt beer, men's beery piss, the stale of ferment.

Ulysses, Episode 8

– Lord love a duck, he said. Look at what I'm standing drinks to! Cold water and gingerpop! Two fellows that would suck whisky off a sore leg.

ib.

– Are you a strict t.t.? says Joe
– Not taking anything between drinks, says I.

ib., Episode 12

– Arrah, give over your bloody codding, Joe, says I. I've a thirst on me I wouldn't sell for half a crown.

ib.

I was blue mouldy for the want of that pint. Declare to God I could hear it hit the pit of my stomach with a click.

ib.

– Dead! says Alf. He's no more dead than you are.
– Maybe so, says Joe. They took the liberty of burying him this morning anyhow.

ib.

And Joe asked him would he have another.
– I will, says he, *a chara*, to show there's no ill feeling.
Gob, he's not as green as he's cabbagelooking.

ib.

To hell with them! [the English] The curse of a goodfornothing God light sideways on the bloody thicklugged sons of whore's gets!

ib.

Twenty thousand of them died in the coffinships. But those that came to the land of the free remember the land of bondage. And they will come again and with a vengeance, no cravers, the sons of Granuaile, the champions of Kathleen ni Houlihan.
– Perfectly true, says Bloom. But my point was ...

ib.

– The French! says the citizen. Set of dancing masters! Do you know what it is! They were never worth a roasted fart to Ireland.

ib.

– Will you try another, citizen? says Joe.
– Yes, sir, says he. I will.
– You? says Joe.
– Beholden to you, Joe, says I. May your shadow never grow less.
– Repeat that dose, says Joe.

ib.

– Show us over the drink, says I. Which is which?
– That's mine, says Joe, as the devil said to the dead policeman.

ib.

Who made those allegations? says Alf.
I, says Joe. I'm the alligator.

ib.

– Do you call that a man? says the citizen.
– I wonder did he ever put it out of sight, says Joe.
– Well, there were two children born anyhow, says Jack Power.
– And who does he suspect? says the citizen

ib.

But begob I was just lowering the heel of the pint when I saw the citizen getting up to waddle to the door, puffing and blowing with the dropsy, and he cursing the curse of Cromwell on him, bell, book and candle in Irish, spitting and spatting out of him and Joe and little Alf round him like a leprechaun trying to peacify him.

ib.

Arrah, sit down on the parliamentary side of your arse for Christ' sake and don't be making a public exhibition of yourself. Jesus, there's always some bloody clown or other kicking up a bloody murder about bloody nothing. Gob, it'd turn the porter sour in your guts, so it would.

ib.

Religion

Who is the funny fellow who declines to go to church
Since pope and priest and parson left the poor man in the
lurch?

Poems and Epiphanies, 'Dooleysprudence'

'And what do you think but there he was, sitting up by himself
in the dark in his confession-box, wide-awake and
laughing-like softly to himself?' ... and I knew that the old
priest was lying still in his coffin as we had seen him, solemn
and truculent in death, an idle chalice on his breast.

Dubliners, 'The Sisters'

'O, pa!' he cried. 'Don't beat me, pa! And I'll ... I'll say a *Hail
Mary* for you ... I'll say a *Hail Mary* for you, pa, if you don't
beat me ... I'll say a *Hail Mary* ...'

ib., 'Counterparts'

Her beliefs were not extravagant. She believed steadily in the
Sacred Heart as the most generally useful of all Catholic
devotions and approved of the sacraments. Her faith was
bounded by her kitchen but, if she was put to it, she could
believe also in the banshee and in the Holy Ghost.

ib., 'Grace'

'Well, I have looked into my accounts. I find this wrong and
this wrong. But with God's grace, I will rectify this and this. I
will set right my accounts.'

ib.

God and religion before everything! Dante cried. God and
religion before the world!

A Portrait of the Artist as a Young Man, ch. 1

– No God for Ireland! he cried. We have had too much God in
Ireland. Away with God!
– Blasphemer! Devil! screamed Dante, starting to her feet and
almost spitting in his face.

ib.

And the damned are so utterly bound and helpless that, as a blessed saint, saint Anselm, writes in his book on similitudes, they are not even able to remove from the eye a worm that gnaws it.

ib., ch. 3

He knelt among them, happy and shy. The altar was heaped with fragrant masses of white flowers: and in the morning light the pale flames of the candles among the white flowers were clear and silent as his own soul.

ib.

He thought of them [priests] as men who washed their bodies briskly with cold water and wore clean cold linen.

ib., ch. 4

He had seen himself, a young and silentmannered priest, entering a confessional swiftly, ascending the altar steps, incensing, genuflecting, accomplishing the vague acts of the priesthood which pleased him by reason of their semblance of reality and of their distance from it.

ib.

He would never swing the thurible before the tabernacle as priest. His destiny was to be elusive of social or religious orders ... wandering among the snares of the world.

ib.

– Did the idea ever occur to you, Cranly asked, that Jesus was not what he pretended to be?
– The first person to whom that idea occurred, Stephen answered, was Jesus himself.

ib., ch. 5

I fear more than that [damnation] the chemical action which would be set up in my soul by a false homage to a symbol behind which are massed twenty centuries of authority and veneration.

ib.

– Then, said Cranly, you do not intend to become a protestant?
– I said that I had lost the faith, Stephen answered, but not that I had lost selfrespect. What kind of liberation would that be to forsake an absurdity which is logical and coherent and to embrace one which is illogical and incoherent?

ib.

Stately, plump Buck Mulligan came from the stairhead,
bearing a bowl of lather on which a mirror and a razor lay
crossed. A yellow dressinggown, ungirdled, was sustained
gently behind him by the mild morning air. He held the bowl
aloft and intoned:
– *Introibo ad altare Dei.*

Ulysses, Episode 1

All human history moves towards one great goal, the
manifestation of God.
  Stephen jerked his thumb towards the window, saying:
– That is God.
  Hooray! Ay! Whrrwhee!
– What? Mr Deasy asked.
– A shout in the street, Stephen answered, shrugging his
shoulders.

ib., Episode 2

Buddha their god lying on his side in the museum. Taking it
easy with hand under his cheek. Jossticks burning. Not like
Ecce Homo. Crown of thorns and cross.

ib., Episode 5

Now I bet it makes them feel happy. Lollipop. It does. Yes,
bread of angels it's called. There's a big idea behind it, kind of
kingdom of God is within you feel.

ib.

Thing is if you really believe it. Lourdes cure, waters of
oblivion, and the Knock apparition, statues bleeding. Old
fellow asleep near that confessionbox. Hence those snores.
Blind faith.

ib.

The priest was rinsing out the chalice: then he tossed off the
dregs smartly. Wine. Makes it more aristocratic than for
example if he drank what they are used to Guinness's porter or
some temperance beverage.

ib.

Confession. Everyone wants to. Then I will tell you all.
Penance. Punish me, please. Great weapon in their hands.
More than doctor or solicitor.

ib.

The resurrection and the life. That last day idea. Knocking them all up out of their graves ... Get up! Last day! Then every fellow mousing around for his liver and his lights and the rest of his traps. Find damn all of himself that morning.

ib., Episode 6

It was idyllic: and Father Conmee reflected on the providence of the Creator who had made turf to be in bogs whence men might dig it out and bring it to town and hamlet to make fires in the houses of poor people.

ib., Episode 10

A flushed young man came from a gap of a hedge and after him came a young woman with wild nodding daisies in her hand. The young man raised his cap abruptly: the young woman abruptly bent and with slow care detached from her light skirt a clinging twig.
Father Conmee blessed both gravely and turned the page of his breviary. *Sin.*

ib.

– And the Saviour was a jew and his father was a jew. Your God.
– He had no father, says Martin. That'll do now. Drive ahead.
– Whose God? says the citizen.
– Well, his uncle was a jew, says he. Your God was a jew. Christ was a jew like me.
    Gob, the citizen made a plunge back into the shop.
– By Jesus, says he, I'll brain that bloody jewman for using the holy name. By Jesus, I'll crucify him so I will.

ib., Episode 12

The Deity ain't no nickle dime bumshow. I put it to you that he's on the square and a corking fine business proposition. He's the grandest thing yet and don't you forget it. Shout salvation in King Jesus.

ib., Episode 15

My mind rejects the whole present social order and Christianity – home, the recognised virtues, classes of life, and religious doctrines.

Letter, 29 August 1904

But why should I have brought Nora to a priest or a lawyer to make her swear away her life to me? And why should I superimpose on my child the very troublesome burden of belief which my father and mother superimposed on me?

Letter, 2 or 3 May 1905

For my part I believe that to establish the church in full power again in Europe would mean a renewal of the Inquisition.

Letter, 12 August 1906

I see nothing on every side of me but the image of the adulterous priest and his servants.

Letter, 27 October 1909

I confess that I do not see what good it does to fulminate against the English tyranny while the Roman tyranny occupies the palace of the soul.

Critical Writings of James Joyce, p. 173

The Church has made inroads everywhere, so that we are in fact becoming a bourgeois nation, with the Church supplying the aristocracy ... and I do not see much hope for us intellectually. Once the Church is in command she will devour everything.

Quoted in A. Power, *Conversations with James Joyce,* p. 65

In the nineteenth century, in the full tide of rationalistic positivism and equal democratic rights for everyone, it [the Catholic Church] proclaims the dogma of the infallibility of the head of the Church and also that of the Immaculate Conception.

Quoted in F. Budgen, *Further Recollections of James Joyce*

[To a friend who asked him, 'What do you think of the next life?']
I don't think much of this one.

Quoted in R. Ellmann, *James Joyce,* ch. 25

In Ireland Catholicism is black magic.

ih, ch. 37

Love

Gentle lady, do not sing
Sad songs about the end of love;
Lay aside sadness and sing
How love that passes is enough.

Chamber Music, 28

I thought little of the future. I did not know whether I would
ever speak to her or not or, if I spoke to her, how I could tell
her of my confused adoration. But my body was like a harp
and her words and gestures were like fingers running upon the
wires.

Dubliners, 'Araby'

Some mothers would be content to patch up such an affair for
a sum of money; she had known cases of it. But she would not
do so. For her only one reparation could make up for the loss
of her daughter's honour: marriage.

ib., 'The Boarding House'

What could he do now but marry her or run away? He could
not brazen it out. The affair would be sure to be talked of and
his employer would be certain to hear of it. Dublin is such a
small city: everyone knows everyone else's business.

ib.

At last she heard her mother calling. She started to her feet and
ran to the banisters.
– Polly! Polly!
– Yes, mamma?
– Come down, dear. Mr Doran wants to speak to you. Then she
remembered what she had been waiting for.

ib.

He looked down the slope and, at the base, in the shadow of
the wall of the park, he saw some human figures lying. Those
venal and furtive loves filled him with despair. He gnawed the
rectitude of his life; he felt that he had been outcast from life's
feast.

ib., 'A Painful Case'

But the young men whom she met were ordinary and she gave them no encouragement, trying to console her romantic desires by eating a great deal of Turkish Delight in secret. However, when she drew near the limit and her friends began to loosen their tongues about her she silenced them by marrying Mr Kearney, who was a bootmaker on Ormond Quay.

ib., 'A Mother'

Like the tender fires of stars moments of their life together, that no one knew of or would ever know of, broke upon and illumined his memory. He longed to recall to her those moments, to make her forget the years of their dull existence together and remember only their moments of ecstasy.

ib., 'The Dead'

– And did you not tell him to go back? asked Gabriel.
– I implored of him to go home at once and told him he would get his death in the rain. But he said he did not want to live. I can see his eyes as well as well! He was standing at the end of the wall where there was a tree.

ib.

So she had had that romance in her life: a man had died for her sake. It hardly pained him now to think how poor a part he, her husband, had played in her life.

ib.

He thought of how she who lay beside him had locked in her heart for so many years that image of her lover's eyes when he had told her that he did not wish to live ... Generous tears filled Gabriel's eyes.

ib.

He closed his eyes, surrendering himself to her, body and mind, conscious of nothing in the world but the dark pressure of her softly parting lips. They pressed upon his brain as upon his lips as though they were the vehicle of a vague speech; and between them he felt an unknown and timid pressure, darker than the swoon of sin, softer than sound or odour.

A Portrait of the Artist as a Young Man, ch. 2

RICHARD: Because in the very core of my ignoble heart I longed to be betrayed by you and by her – in the dark, in the night – secretly, meanly, craftily. By you, my best friend, and by her.

Exiles, Act 2

I am sure that no law made by man is sacred before the impulse of passion.

ib.

Touch me. Soft eyes. Soft soft soft hand. I am lonely here. O, touch me soon, now. What is that word known to all men? I am quiet here alone. Sad too. Touch, touch me.

Ulysses, Episode 3

Assumed dongiovannism will not save him. No later undoing will undo the first undoing. The tusk of the boar has wounded him there where love lies ableeding.

ib., Episode 9

Love loves to love love. Nurse loves the new chemist. Constable 14A loves Mary Kelly. Gerty MacDowell loves the boy that has the bicycle. M.B. loves a fair gentleman. Li Chi Han lovey up kissy Cha Pu Chow. Jumbo, the elephant, loves Alice, the elephant.

ib., Episode 12

And then a rocket sprang and bang shot blind blank and O! then the Roman candle burst and it was like a sigh of O! and everyone cried O! O! in raptures and it gushed out of it a stream of rain gold hair threads and they shed and ah! they were all greeny dewy stars falling with golden, O so lovely, O, soft, sweet, soft!

ib., Episode 13

Greater love than this, he said, no man hath that a man lay down his wife for his friend. Go thou and do likewise. Thus, or words to that effect, saith Zarathustra, sometime regius professor of French letters to the university of Oxtail.

ib., Episode 14

and how he kissed me under the Moorish wall and I thought well as well him as another and then I asked him with my eyes to ask again yes and then he asked me would I yes to say yes my mountain flower and first I put my arms around him yes and drew him down to me so he could feel my breasts all perfume yes and his heart was going like mad and yes I said yes I will Yes.

ib., Episode 18

as appi as a oneysucker or a baskerboy on the Libido, with
Floh biting his leg thigh and Luse lugging his luff leg and Bieni
bussing him under his bonnet and Vespatilla blowing cosy
fond tutties up the allabroad length of the large of his smalls.

Finnegans Wake, p. 417

win me, woo me, wed me, ah weary me!

ib., p. 556

I see you in a hundred poses, grotesque, shameful, virginal,
languorous. Give yourself to me, dearest, all, all when we meet.

Letter, 22 August 1909

I remember the first night in Pola when in the tumult of our
embraces you used a certain word. It was a word of
provocation, of invitation and I can see your face over me (you
were *over* me that night) as you murmured it. There was
madness in *your* eyes too and as for me if hell had been
waiting for me the moment after I could not have held back
from you.

Letter, 2 September 1909

Love is a cursed nuisance especially when coupled with lust
also.

Letter, 7 September 1909

I have felt her soul tremble beside mine, and have spoken her
name softly to the night, and have wept to see the beauty of
the world passing like a dream behind her eyes.

Letter, 19 November 1909

O my dearest, if you would only turn to me even now and
read that terrible book [*Ulysses*] which has now broken the
heart in my breast and take me to yourself alone to do with me
what you will!

Letter, April 1922

When I hear the word 'love' I feel like puking.

Quoted in R. Ellmann, *James Joyce*, ch. 34

Language

Every night as I gazed up at the window I said softly to myself the word paralysis. It had always sounded strangely in my ears, like the word gnomon in the Euclid and the word simony in the Catechism.

Dubliners, 'The Sisters'

– Well, you see, I'm like the famous Mrs Cassidy, who is reported to have said: *Now, Mary Grimes, if I don't take it, make me take it, for I feel I want it.*
His hot face had leaned forward a little too confidentially and he had assumed a very low Dublin accent so that the young ladies, with one instinct, received his speech in silence.

ib., 'The Dead'

He read Skeat's *Etymological Dictionary* by the hour and his mind, which had from the first been only too submissive to the infant sense of wonder, was often hypnotized by the most commonplace conversation. People seemed to him strangely ignorant of the value of the words they used so glibly.

Stephen Hero, p. 26

Words which he did not understand he said over and over to himself till he had learnt them by heart: and through them he had glimpses of the real world about him.

A Portrait of the Artist as a Young Man, ch. 2

– A day of dappled seaborne clouds.
The phrase and the day and the scene harmonised in a chord.
Words. Was it their colours?

ib., ch. 4

Or was it that, being as weak of sight as he was shy of mind, he drew less pleasure from the reflection of the glowing sensible world through the prism of a language manycoloured and richly storied than from the contemplation of an inner world of individual emotions mirrored perfectly in a lucid periodic prose?

ib.

His language [English], so familiar and so foreign, will always be for me an acquired speech. I have not made or accepted its words. My voice holds them at bay. My soul frets in the shadow of his language.

ib., ch. 5

Cranly's speech, unlike that of Davin, had neither rare phrases of Elizabethan English nor quaintly turned versions of Irish idioms. Its drawl was an echo of the quays of Dublin given back by a bleak decaying seaport.

ib.

I fear those big words, Stephen said, which make us so unhappy.

Ulysses, Episode 2

– Metempsychosis, he said, frowning. It's Greek: from the Greek. That means the transmigration of souls.
– O, rocks! she said. Tell us in plain words.

ib., Episode 4

Lady Sylvester Elmshade, Mrs Barbara Lovebirch, Mrs Poll Ash, Mrs Holly Hazeleyes, Miss Daphne Bays, Miss Dorothy Canebrake, Mrs Clyde Twelvetrees, Mrs Roean Greene, Mrs Helen Vinegladding, Miss Virginia Creeper, Miss Gladys Beech, Miss Olive Garth, Miss Blanche Maple, Mrs Maud Mahogany, Miss Myra Myrtle, Miss Priscilla Elderflower, Miss Bee Honeysuckle, Miss Grace Poplar

ib., Episode 12

The summer evening had begun to fold the world in its mysterious embrace. Far away in the west the sun was setting and the last glow of all too fleeting day lingered lovingly on sea and strand, on the proud promontory of dear old Howth guarding as ever the waters of the bay, on the weedgrown rocks along Sandymount shore and, last but not least, on the quiet church where there streamed forth at times upon the stillness the voice of prayer to her who is in her pure radiance a beacon ever to the stormtossed heart of man, Mary, star of the sea.

ib., Episode 13

this is nat language at any sinse of the world

Finnegans Wake, p. 83

what do you think Vulgariano did but study with stolen fruit how cutely to copy all their various styles of signature so as one day to utter an epical forged cheque on the public

ib., p. 181

And his derry's own drawl and his corksown blather and his doubling stutter and his gullaway swank.

ib., p. 197

his face glows green, his hair greys white, his bleyes bcome broon to suite his cultic twalette

ib., p. 344

Are we speachin d'anglas landage or are you sprakin sea Djoytsch?

ib., p. 485

I'd like a language which is above all languages, a language to which all will do service. I cannot express myself in English without enclosing myself in a tradition.

Letter, 12 July 1905

If the Irish programme did not insist on the Irish language I suppose I could call myself a nationalist.

Letter, 6 November 1906

Is it affectation or impotence of the English that they can make no attempt to pronounce any language but their own.

Letter, 13 November 1906

One great part of every human existence is passed in a state which cannot be rendered sensible by the use of wideawake language, cutanddry grammar and goahead plot.

Letter, 21 December 1926

The Irish, condemned to express themselves in a language not their own, have stamped on it the mark of their own genius and compete for glory with the civilised nations. This is then called English literature.

Quoted in R. Ellmann, *James Joyce*, ch. 13

Je suis au bout de l'anglais. [I'm at the end of English]

ib., ch. 31

Leopold Bloom

He liked thick giblet soup, nutty gizzards, a stuffed roast heart, liverslices fried with crustcrumbs, fried hencods' roes. Most of all he liked grilled mutton kidneys which gave to his palate a fine tang of faintly scented urine.

Ulysses, Episode 4

Quietly he read, restraining himself, the first column and, yielding but resisting, began the second. Midway, his last resistance yielding, he allowed his bowels to ease themselves quietly as he read, reading still patiently that slight constipation of yesterday quite gone.

ib.

I read in that *Voyages in China* that the Chinese say a white man smells like a corpse. Cremation better. Priests dead against it. Devilling for the other firm.

ib., Episode 6

Plenty to see and hear and feel yet. Feel live warm beings near you. Let them sleep in their maggoty beds. They are not going to get me this innings. Warm beds: warm fullblooded life.

ib.

Mr Bloom walked unheeded along his grove by saddened angels, crosses, broken pillars, family vaults, stone hopes praying with upcast eyes, old Ireland's hearts and hands.

ib.

Silly billies [students]: mob of young cubs yelling their guts out [at a political demonstration] ... Few years' time half of them magistrates and civil servants.

ib., Episode 8

One born every second somewhere. Other dying every second. Since I fed the birds five minutes. Three hundred kicked the bucket. Other three hundred born, washing the blood off, all are washed in the blood of the lamb, bawling maaaaaa.

ib.

Pyramids in sand. Built on bread and onions. Slaves Chinese wall. Babylon. Big stones left. Round towers. Rest rubble, sprawling suburbs, jerrybuilt.

ib.

Don't eat a beefsteak. If you do the eyes of that cow pursue you through all eternity. They say it's [vegetarianism] healthier. Windandwatery though. Tried it. Keep you on the run all day.

ib.

I wouldn't be surprised if it was that kind of food [vegetarianism] you see produces the like waves of the brain the poetical. For example one of those policemen sweating Irish stew into their shirts you couldn't squeeze a line of poetry out of him.

ib.

I was happier then. Or was that I? Or am I now I? Twentyeight I was. She twentythree. When we left Lombard street west something changed. Could never like it again after [death of baby] Rudy. Can't bring back time. Like holding water in your hand.

ib.

His heart astir he pushed in the door of the Burton restaurant. Stink gripped his trembling breath: pungent meatjuice, slush of greens. See the animals feed.
Men, men, men.
Perched on high stools by the bar, hats shoved back, at the tables calling for more bread no charge, swilling, wolfing, gobfuls of sloppy food, their eyes bulging, wiping wetted moustaches.

ib.

She kissed me. I was kissed. All yielding she tossed my hair. Kissed, she kissed me.
Me. And me now.

ib.

He's been known to put his hand down too to help a fellow. Give the devil his due, O Bloom has his good points.

ib.

I declare to my antimacassar if you took up a straw from the
bloody floor and if you said to Bloom: *Look at, Bloom. Do you
see that straw? That's a straw.* Declare to my aunt he'd talk
about it for an hour so he would and talk steady.

ib., Episode 12

– a nation? says Bloom. A nation is the same people living in
the same place.
– By God, then, says Ned, laughing, if that's so I'm a nation for
I'm living in the same place for the past five years.
   So of course everyone had the laugh at Bloom and says he,
trying to muck out of it:
– Or also living in different places.
– That covers my case, says Joe.
– What is your nation if I may ask? says the citizen.
– Ireland, says Bloom. I was born here. Ireland.

ib.

That's not life for men and women, insult and hatred. And
everybody knows that it's the very opposite of that that is
really life.
– What? says Alf.
– Love, says Bloom. I mean the opposite of hatred.

ib.

– And I belong to a race too, says Bloom, that is hated and
persecuted. Also now. This very moment. This very instant.
Gob, he near burnt his fingers with the butt of his old cigar.

ib.

And they beheld Him even Him, ben Bloom Elijah, amid
clouds of angels ascend to the glory of the brightness at an
angle of fortyfive degrees over Donohoe's in Little Green street
like a shot off a shovel.

ib.

Pray for us. And pray for us. And pray for us. Good idea the
repetition. Same thing with ads. Buy from us. And buy from us.

ib., Episode 13

Love, lie and be handsome for tomorrow we die.

ib.

And the traveller Leopold went into the castle for to rest him for a space being sore of limb after many marches environing in divers lands and sometimes venery.

ib., Episode 14

and now sir Leopold that had of his body no manchild for an heir looked upon him his friend's son and was shut up in sorrow for his forepast happiness and as sad he was that him failed a son of such gentle courage.

ib.

so grieved he also in no less measure for young Stephen for that he lived riotously with those wastrels and murdered his goods with whores.

ib.

I stand for ... three acres and a cow for all children of nature. Saloon motor hearses. Compulsory manual labour for all. All parks open to the public day and night. Electric dishscrubbers. Tuberculosis, lunacy, war and mendicancy must now cease. General amnesty, weekly carnival with masked license, bonuses for all, esperanto the universal language with universal brotherhood.

ib., Episode 15

No more patriotism of barspongers and dropsical impostors.

ib.

The poor man starves while they are gassing their royal mountain stags or shooting peasants and phartridges in their purblind pomp of pelf and power.

ib.

What, reduced to their simplest reciprocal form, were Bloom's thoughts about Stephen's thoughts about Bloom and about Stephen's thoughts about Bloom's thoughts about Stephen?
 He thought that he thought that he was a jew whereas he knew that he knew that he knew that he was not.

ib., Episode 17

What did his limbs, when gradually extended, encounter?
 New clean bedlinen, additional odours, the presence of a human form, female, hers, the imprint of a human form, male, not his.

ib.

From outrage (matrimony) to outrage (adultery) there arose
nought but outrage (copulation) yet the matrimonial violator
of the matrimonially violated had not been outraged by the
adulterous violator of the adulterously violated.

ib.

He kissed the plump mellow yellow smellow melons of her
rump, on each plump melonous hemisphere, in their mellow
yellow furrow, with obscure prolonged provocative
melonsmellonous osculation.

ib.

that was why we had the standup row over politics he began it
not me when he said Our Lord being a carpenter at last he
made me cry of course a woman is so sensitive about
everything I was fuming with myself after for giving in only
for I knew he was gone on me and the first socialist he said He
was

ib., Episode 18

hes mad on the subject of drawers thats plain to be seen always
skeezing at those brazenfaced things on the bicycles with their
skirts blowing up to their navels

ib.

Bloom's justness and reasonableness should grow in interest.
As the day wears on Bloom should overshadow them all.

Quoted in F. Budgen, *James Joyce and the Making of 'Ulysses'*

Philosophy

Who is the tranquil gentleman who won't salute the State
Or serve Nebuchadnezzar or proletariat
But thinks that every son of man has quite enough to do
To paddle down the stream of life his personal canoe?

Poems and Epiphanies, 'Dooleysprudence'

A sparrow under the wheels of Juggernaut, shaking shaker of
the earth! Please, mister God, big mister God! Goodbye, big
world!

Giacomo Joyce

One by one they were all becoming shades. Better pass boldly
into that other world, in the full glory of some passion, than
fade and wither dismally with age.

Dubliners, 'The Dead'

His own identity was fading out into a grey impalpable world:
the solid world itself which these dead had one time reared
and lived in was dissolving and dwindling.

ib.

His soul swooned slowly as he heard the snow falling faintly
through the universe and faintly falling, like the descent of
their last end, upon all the living and the dead.

ib.

What did it profit a man to gain the whole world if he lost his
soul? At last he had understood: and human life lay around
him, a plain of peace whereon antlike men laboured in
brotherhood, their dead sleeping under quiet mounds.

A Portrait of the Artist as a Young Man, ch. 3

White pudding and eggs and sausages and cups of tea. How
simple and beautiful was life after all! And life lay all before
him.

ib.

To live, to err, to fall, to triumph, to recreate life out of life!

ib., ch. 4

Welcome, O life! I go to encounter for the millionth time the reality of experience and to forge in the smithy of my soul the uncreated conscience of my race.

ib., ch. 5

There's good times coming still.
BERTHA: No, Brigid, that time comes once in a lifetime. The rest of life is good for nothing except to remember that time.

Exiles, Act 3

Signatures of all things I am here to read, seaspawn and seawrack, the nearing tide, that rusty boot.

Ulysses, Episode 3

If we were all suddenly somebody else.

ib., Episode 6

Hold to the now, the here, through which all future plunges to the past.

ib., Episode 9

Wait. Five months. Molecules all change. I am other I now.

ib.

Agenbite of inwit: remorse of conscience. It is an age of exhausted whoredom groping for its god.

ib.

Part. The moment is now. Where then? If Socrates leave his house today, if Judas go forth tonight. Why? That lies in space which I in time must come to, ineluctably.

ib.

(*He taps his brow.*) But in here it is I must kill the priest and the king.

ib., Episode 15

who was the first person in the universe before there was anybody that made it all who ah that they [atheists] don't know neither do I so there you are they might as well try to stop the sun from shining tomorrow

ib., Episode 18

His howd feeled heavy, his hoddit did shake. (There was a
wall of course in erection) Dimb! He stottered from the latter.
Damb! He was dud. Dumb! ... Macool, Macool, orra whyi
deed ye die? of a trying thirstay mourning?

Finnegans Wake, p. 6

Become a bitskin more wiseable, as if I were you.

ib., p. 16

It darkles, (tinct, tint) all this our funnaminal world. You
marshpond by ruodmark verge is visited by the tide.
Alvemmarea! We are circumveiloped by obscuritads.

ib., p. 244

In the buginning is the woid, in the muddle is the sounddance
and thereinofter you're in the unbewised again

ib., p. 378

Where are we at all? and whenabouts in the name of space? I
don't understand. I fail to say. I dearsee you too.

ib., p. 558

They [anarchists] decline to interfere in politics or religion or
legal questions. They do not desire the conquest of public
powers, which, they say, only serve in the end to support the
middle-class government ... Their objections to
parliamentarianism seem to me well-founded.

Letter, 9 October 1906

Rome reminds me of a man who lives by exhibiting to
travellers his grandmother's corpse.

ib.

How sad life is, from one disillusion to another!

Letter, 23 December 1909

O shite and onions! When is this bloody state of affairs going to
end.

Letter, 3 January 1920

Children may just as well play as not. The ogre will come in
any case.

Letter, 16 October 1925

My political faith can be expressed in a word: Monarchies, constitutional or unconstitutional, disgust me. Kings are mountebanks.

Quoted in H. Gorman, *James Joyce*

'May I kiss the hand that wrote *Ulysses*?' [A young admirer asked Joyce in a Zurich street]
'No, it did lots of other things too.'

Quoted in R. Ellmann, *James Joyce*, ch. 7

Naturally, I can't approve of the act of the revolutionary who tosses a bomb in a theatre to destroy the king and his children. On the other hand, have those states behaved any better which have drowned the world in a blood-bath?

ib., ch. 25

As for psychoanalysis, it's neither more nor less than blackmail.

ib., ch. 30

White wine is like electricity. Red wine looks and tastes like a liquefied beefsteak.

Quoted in F. Budgen, *James Joyce and the Making of 'Ulysses'*

[Responding to a painter's assertion that he wanted to capture Joyce's soul in his portrait.]
Get the poet's soul of your mind and see that you paint my cravat properly.

Quoted in F. Budgen, *Further Recollections of James Joyce*

[Asked 'What do you think about life?']
'I don't think about it.'

Quoted in R. Ellmann, *James Joyce*, ch. 8

Why all this fuss and bother about the mystery of the unconscious? What about the mystery of the conscious? What do they know about that?

Quoted in F. Budgen, *James Joyce and the Making of 'Ulysses'*

Chance furnishes me what I need. I am like a man who stumbles along; my foot strikes something, I bend over and it is exactly what I want.

Quoted in B. Maddox, *Nora*

Conclusions

Perhaps she had not told him all the story.

Dubliners, 'The Dead'

I hear the ruin of all space, shattered glass and toppling masonry, and time one livid final flame.

Ulysses, Episode 2

Every life is many days, day after day. We walk through ourselves, meeting robbers, ghosts, giants, old men, young men, wives, widows, brothers-in-love, but always meeting ourselves.

ib., Episode 9

Wharnow are alle her childer, say? In kingdome gone or power to come or gloria be to them farther? Allalivial allalluvial! Some here, more no more, more again lost alla stranger.

Finnegans Wake, p. 213

Quiet takes back her folded fields. Tranquille thanks. Adew.

ib., p. 214

– Three quarks for Muster Mark!
Sure he hasn't got much of a bark
And sure any he has it's all beside the mark.

ib., p. 383

Toborrow and toburrow and tobarrow! That's our crass, hairy and evergrim life, till one finel howdiedow Bouncer Naster raps on the bell with a bone and his stinkers stank behind him with the sceptre and the hourglass.

ib., p. 455

Eftsoon so too will our own sphoenix spark spirt his spyre and sunward stride the rampante flambe. Ay, already the sombrer opacities of the gloom are sphanished!

ib., p. 473

Hold to! Now! Win out, ye devil ye! The silent cock shall crow at last. The west shall shake the east awake. Walk while ye have the night for morn, lighbreakfastbringer, morroweth whereon every past shall full fost sleep. Amain.

ib.

Mememormee!

ib., p. 627

Yes, tid. There's where. First. We pass through grass behush the bush to. Whish! A gull. Gulls. Far calls. Coming, far! End here. Us here. Us then. Finn, again! Take. Bussoftlhee, mememormee! Till thousendsthee. Lps. The keys to. Given! A way a lone a last a long the

ib., p. 628